P9-DGB-602

Author
Bill Harris

Photography
Ric Pattison

Designer
Teddy Hartshorn

Editors
Gill Waugh
Pauline Graham

Commissioning Editor
Trevor Hall

Publishing Director
David Gibbon

Production Director
Gerald Hughes

ACKNOWLEDGMENT
The publisher wishes to thank all the individuals and
organizations who so willingly provided assistance, as
well as access to properties, throughout the
preparation and photography for this book.

Library of Congress Cataloging-in-Publication Data

Harris, Bill, 1933
        Grand homes of the Mid-Atlantic States.

1. Dwellings—Middle Atlantic States—Pictorial
works.   2. Historic buildings—Middle Atlantic States—
Pictorial works.   3. Middle Atlantic States—
Description and travel—Views.   I. Title.
F106.H24   1989   728.8'3'0974   89–462
ISBN 0 517 62375 7

CLB 2160
© 1989 Colour Library Books Ltd., Godalming, Surrey, England.
Colour separation by Hong Kong Graphic Arts Ltd., Hong Kong.
This 1989 edition published by Crescent Books,
distributed by Crown Publishers, Inc.,
225 Park Avenue South, New York, New York 10003.
Printed and bound in Hong Kong.
ISBN 0 517 62375 7
h g f e d c b a

GRAND HOMES
OF THE
MID ATLANTIC

Text by
BILL HARRIS

Photography by
RIC PATTISON

CRESCENT BOOKS
NEW YORK

One of the great points of pride among Americans is that our roots are generally spread out. "I'm English-German-Swedish-and-Greek," one might tell you. Another will confess to being a mixture of Italian and Irish, or Spanish and Chinese. It's the same with our houses. In most parts of the world, it is usually possible to look at a building and know instantly what style it is, and just as quickly to determine its age. But in America things are often different. And the differences are what make our historic houses so endlessly fascinating. Especially in the states between New England and the Old South – the heart of the original Colonial America known as the Middle Atlantic States.

The roots of American architecture are in England, of course, but the Dutch in New York, the Swedes in Delaware, the Germans in Pennsylvania and other Europeans who lived among them added their own ideas to the notions of what a good house should look like. And as fashion changed, so did many of our old houses, with the result that most of them tell the story not only of the generation that built them, but of every generation that followed.

But if American history lives in its houses, the early chapters are missing. Except for reconstructions, we have no examples of the way our ancestors lived when they first began arriving here from England. It's a romantic notion that the first colonists took their inspiration from the Indians and lived in log cabins. The fact is that the Indians themselves never thought of building houses from logs until well into the eighteenth century, and they got the idea from the Europeans. It originally came to America from Sweden in 1643 with colonists who settled along the Delaware River.

The earliest houses built in the American wilderness were adaptations of English shepherds' huts, and these were quickly replaced by cottages, also based on English models. But while they were perfectly adequate in the Old Country, the summers are warmer and the winters colder on this side of the Atlantic, and the variations between the seasons caused the exposed frames of the half-timbered buildings to expand and contract. The draft-producing cracks that resulted sent builders back to the drawing board, and they began covering their work with shingles and clapboards. The English models also gave these early homes thatched roofs, but the American climate caused them to rot quickly and builders responded by substituting shingles for straw. Despite these adaptations, they never strayed far from the original inspiration provided by the houses they left behind in England.

Americans who travel abroad usually come back with the impression that the early American versions of English housing were influenced as much by the almost unlimited availability of wood for construction as by the climate. There are very few seventeenth-century wood frame houses left in England these days, but in the early part of that century, when Englishmen began pulling up stakes and leaving for America, wood was the building material of choice for the middle classes. The fashion changed as shipbuilders cleared forests in response to the demands of the King's Navy for better wooden ships. The preference for wooden buildings vanished almost completely after the Great Fire in 1666, which made Englishmen feel more secure in houses made of brick or stone.

Transplanted Englishmen in America, struggling for survival and learning about their new surroundings, didn't begin to create larger houses until a full century after the first of them arrived, and the first houses that could be called "American" appeared in New England. The first generations of immigrants built plainly and economically, but gradually their descendants began adding rooms, second stories, even decorative elements the early Puritans would have considered frivolous. But simplicity was still the most important rule to live by, and wood the only material to build with. Then the Dutch, who spread out along the Hudson River Valley, gave them something new to think about.

Brick was easily available in upstate New York and northern New Jersey, and the Dutch, who had lived in brick houses back home, naturally favored the more durable material over wood. Their New Amsterdam houses featured brick laid in Flemish bond, with headers and stretchers alternating, and stepped gables defining the roof line. In places where brick was too costly, they used fieldstone and faced the gables with clapboarding. Neither style was well-known in England, but New Englanders saw their advantages and by mid-century, they began incorporating some of the ideas into their own houses.

But there were other influences at work in New York and New Jersey, too. Many of the settlers brought to America by the Dutch West India Company were Waloons from southern Belgium. They shared some of the Dutch ideas about building, but added an important refinement in the form of gambrel roofs, which included a ridge and gave two pitches to the normal sloped roof. It was a widely-copied idea because it allowed more headroom in the upper floor. The style, which architectural historians call Flemish Colonial, is usually credited to the Dutch. And though it was introduced through Long Island and northern New Jersey, it was adopted all over New England as well, and sometimes is considered a Massachusetts innovation.

But there was innovation in every colony. The Germans who joined the English Quakers in Pennsylvania brought some solid ideas with them and favored stone houses like the ones they had known along the Rhine. Their English neighbors were building houses with massive chimneys at the ends, but the Germans preferred to have a center chimney, which was smaller than the English versions because it served a single fireplace in the kitchen, far and away the most important room in the house. They also brought a new idea in silhouettes with the steep, single-sloped pent roof. The German ideas were assimilated into the Middle Atlantic scene even more quickly than the Germans themselves. But they, too, were willing to adapt to new building ideas. The Swedes in the Delaware Valley had built two- and three-room log houses which impressed William Penn enough for him to recommend them to people who signed up for passage to Pennsylvania. The Germans took his advice to heart, even though they preferred stone

to logs for the house itself, and they were especially impressed by the Swedish innovation of corner fireplaces in each room, an idea that appealed to their inbred sense of practicality, and one that eventually spread to all the colonies.

Newcomers from England, meanwhile, brought a new style to Pennsylvania in the early part of the eighteenth century. It started an American fashion still treasured under the name "Georgian." The style didn't arrive full-blown, but evolved over the first two or three decades of the century. It had begun in London with the influence of Inigo Jones and Sir Christopher Wren, who themselves had been influenced by the buildings of Renaissance Italy. When medieval London was destroyed in the Great Fire of 1666, the city that rose from the ashes was orderly, compact and, in the opinion of most, admirable. It was a style that worked unusually well in city houses, and Philadelphia, the newest city in America at the time, was doing all it could to emulate the new London. The other colonies that were already established weren't welcoming nearly as many English newcomers, and were slower in catching up with the new style. But over time, as merchants traveled up and down the coast, the new ideas began appearing everywhere.

In England, meanwhile, they were spreading outward from London, and huge Italianate villas, following the basic ideas of architect Andrea Palladio, began appearing all over the countryside. But while they might have been considered homey in sunny Italy, they didn't adapt well to the damp English climate, and many an eighteenth-century manor, though stately, was all but uninhabitable. The Americans, faced with an even harsher climate, didn't bother to try keeping up with that part of the new fashion, but it was clear that fashion was important, and Georgian houses became the only proper architectural statement among people trying to make an impression everywhere from South Carolina to Maine. On the other hand, even though everybody was building Georgian houses, a colonist could be taken blindfolded to any other colony and usually identify the place by the local accents added to the basic building style. As Benjamin Franklin pointed out, every colony has its own "peculiar expressions." It was as true in architecture as it was in speech patterns.

The American colonies found a way out of their rough and tumble frontier existence and into a formal gentility with the Georgian Style, which, for all its subtle differences up and down the coast, unified them. Its basic design elements call for a wide, welcoming, paneled doorway, flanked by windows or topped by a windowed transom. The doorway is formalized by pilasters and there is often a large Palladian window above to light the central hallway – another innovation. The other windows, set in an orderly fashion and framed with cornices, are broken into panes and incorporate another idea new in the eighteenth century, counterweighted sashes. The roof line is usually low, and sometimes flat, to support a balustraded deck.

Inside, the walls are paneled, and the rooms arranged around the high entrance hall, whose centerpiece is an elaborate staircase. The floors are made of hardwood, often parqueted, and the doors are framed. The fireplaces are smaller than those in earlier houses, and are usually lined with tile or marble, with elaborately-carved mantles. In Colonial America, it all represented the last word in elegant living. But as in every fashion, the last word is almost never heard. As it evolved, the Georgian house became more decorative and more elegant. Then, suddenly, evolution turned the other way, and in the years just before the signing of the Declaration of Independence, it led to a much plainer fashion known as the Federal Style. But as the exteriors became more severe, the interiors became more lavish and more liveable. Rooms were arranged for the convenience of the people who lived in them rather than following rigid rules. And it set the stage for yet another fashion that would dominate until the middle of the nineteenth century: Greek Revival.

The fashion hit America in 1804 with Benjamin Henry Latrobe's Baltimore Cathedral. Latrobe had worked in England, but like his close friend, Thomas Jefferson, he rebelled against the Anglo-Italian tradition that had been established there and transplanted to America. His first major building, the 1800 Bank of Pennsylvania in Philadelphia, is along the lines of a classic Roman temple as interpreted in England. But for his Roman Catholic cathedral, he turned directly to the Pantheon in Rome for inspiration. And when it inspired more commissions in the Philadelphia area, he turned more and more to the geometrical purity he found in Greek architecture. With Jefferson's backing, he refined his ideas in mansions and public buildings in the new Federal City at Washington, D.C., and America took them to heart. Though Greek Revival's roots are in antiquity, it represented something brand-new and became America's first native architectural movement. It was only natural, after all. The world's newest democracy had turned to the world's oldest for its model.

The Greeks gave us the guidelines, but the revival didn't include any hard and fast rules. Living in a Greek temple might be a culturally uplifting experience, but it doesn't represent solid comfort. Many Americans gave a nod to the new style by adding columned porticoes to the front of their houses but designing the interiors to suit their own lifestyle. Others went all the way, with classical decoration on doorframes and mantles, elaborate cornices and other bows to the noble Greeks, but almost always executed in wood rather than marble. Either way, nothing could be more American than a style that allows such a wide range of individual interpretation. It's no wonder it overshadowed every other style for more than a half-century.

It was also a style that could be easily added to an existing house, and a great many older houses in established areas were modernized and brought up to date with the addition of a few columns and rosettes. And when families began moving West, they took their Greek Revival ideas with them, first into Ohio and Indiana and eventually all the way to California during the 1849 Gold Rush. But by then, a new fashion had taken hold back East. Its roots are in such diverse places as France, Italy and Turkey, but its name takes American architectural development back to England, to the reign of Queen Victoria.

It was probably inevitable. All of the previous styles had been related to classical forms and by the middle of the nineteenth century a new statement was needed. It arrived in the form of Gothic Revival, an old form made new and popularized in England with John Ruskin's book, *The Stones of Venice*. Its chief disciple in America was Andrew Jackson Downing, a horticulturalist who wrote a book in 1841 expounding the revolutionary idea that a house should always be arranged to take advantage of the surrounding landscape. He even went so far as to say that it didn't need orderly arrangements if an irregular shape could enhance the view from inside. No one in America had thought of that before. The classical forms they had been following dictated that any wings attached to a house needed to extend outward along a formal plan. Now Downing was telling them it was just fine, even desirable, for a house to ramble all over the lot as long as it complemented it.

Downing's book, a steady seller for nearly forty years, was illustrated with designs by Alexander Jackson Davis, who was building Gothic cottages and country houses in New York and New Jersey and was influencing other architects as far away as California. He himself was unhappy with what he saw as a movement toward "frippery and gingerbread, which degrades rather than elevates." But he considered himself an architectural rebel, and he kept his peace when other rebels he inspired let their imaginations run full tilt and created romantic, fanciful environments of gables and crockets and a full measure of whimsey. In the final analysis, they created homes that were as much fun to live in as to look at. And they defined an era.

By 1850 was no question that a new era had come, and there was a rush among families who wanted to make the right impression to remake their houses in the new fashion. A great many very fine Greek Revival houses were Gothicized, but most of them survived behind their new facades. Some were even improved. The new fashion allowed carpenters and architects to let their imaginations take them in any any of a dozen different directions. But their creations had one new thing in common: the great houses of the period were all light, airy and roomy. Interior designers and their clients went out of their way to make them cluttered with heavy, dark furnishings, but the houses could take it without losing a shred of their charm.

The earliest versions of the style were relatively simple and intended to be made of stone, but the cost factor moved it quickly along to a movement known as "Carpenter Gothic," inspired by builders with coping saws and vivid imaginations. Eventually the style faded, but the obvious advantage of extra space that could be provided by a free-form plan led to bigger and better houses, and that, in turn, led to a heavier, more elaborate style called "Hudson River Bracketed," whose elaborate towers and balconies seemed to have taken the movement as far as it could go.

But after the Civil War it went even further. Houses were built with turrets and pinnacles, the wooden scrollwork was replaced by more decorative cast iron, mansard roofs became all the rage, and the houses were painted in a riot of pastel colors. Later still they were crowned with towers and arches inspired by Middle Eastern architecture. But the real inspiration was strictly American, even though the era was named for an English queen.

By the time Victoria died in 1901, American architects had already begun looking back at the more formal expressions of Greece and Rome. Chief among them were Stanford White and his partner Charles F. McKim, who were steeped in the Beaux Arts tradition and had studied with the great Boston architect, H.H. Richardson, whose Romanesque buildings in Chicago greatly influenced Louis Sullivan and his pupil Frank Lloyd Wright. McKim and White pushed the Classical Revival forward with their work at Chicago's Columbian Exposition in 1893. But they also influenced a return to the Georgian Style through the Colonial Revival, which sent Americans back to their own roots in search of a better way to live.

It sparked a building boom the like of which the country had never seen before. Because of the boom, real estate values skyrocketed and literally thousands of valuable old houses vanished. New, modern conveniences like electric lights and central heating made it cheaper to replace a house than to bring it up to date. And for the first time, good taste and comfort were not just reserved for the wealthy, and builders concentrated on smaller houses that allowed the middle class to indulge in impressing their neighbors with their houses. Prefabricated houses took the country by storm; even Frank Lloyd Wright got into the act in 1901 with a house that sold for less than $6,000.

The result of all the building is that hundreds of the best examples of America's architectural history have vanished for ever. In the 1960s, Lady Bird Johnson pointed out that in less than thirty years we lost almost half the buildings included in the first Historic American Buildings Survey. And in the thirty years since then, even more have been demolished. But there are rays of hope, and many of them are to be found in these pages. They all tell us something about who we are and where we came from. America's history lives in its houses.

Visitor's Guide

Most of the homes pictured in these pages may be visited, and the majority provide guided tours. Those listed below are open to the public:

New York

George Eastman House, 900 East Avenue, Rochester, N.Y. 14607. (716) 271-3361. (p.11) Open Tuesday through Saturday, 10a.m.-4:30p.m, and on Sunday from 1p.m. The mansion itself is scheduled to reopen in 1990 after extensive renovations. The museum contains the world's most important collection of photographic material. Admission charged.

Millard Fillmore House, 24 Shearer Avenue, East Aurora, N.Y. 14052. (716) 652-4228. (pp.12,13) Open Wednesday, Saturday and Sunday from June through mid-October.

Schuyler Mansion State Historic Site, 32 Catherine Street, Albany, N.Y. 12202. (518) 434-0834. (pp.14,15) Open April through December, Wednesday to Saturday, 10a.m.-5p.m, and on Sunday 1p.m. Call to check for off-season opening hours.

Roosevelt-Vanderbilt National Historic Sites, Route 9, Hyde Park, N.Y. 12538. (914) 229-9115. (pp.16–19) Includes the home of Franklin D. Roosevelt, with its library and museum; the Frederick W. Vanderbilt Mansion; and Val-Kill, the Eleanor Roosevelt home. Open daily April through October; Thursday to Monday, and November through March. Admission charged.

Boscobel, Route 9-D, Garrison-on-Hudson, N.Y. 10524. (914) 265-3638. (pp.20–23) Open daily, except Tuesday, April through October, 9:30a.m.-5p.m. During November, December and March it is open 9:30a.m.-4p.m. Closed January and February. Admission charged.

Montgomery Place, P.O. Box 32, Annandale-on-Hudson, N.Y. 12504. (914) 758-5461. (pp.24–27) (A Historic Hudson Valley property, 150 White Plains Road, Tarrytown, N.Y. 10591.) Open daily, except Tuesday, April through October, 10a.m.-5p.m.; and on weekends during November, December and March. Admission charged.

Van Cortlandt Manor, Route 9, Croton-on-Hudson, N.Y. 10520. (914) 631-8200. (pp.28,29) (A Historic Hudson Valley property, 150 White Plains Road, Tarrytown, N.Y. 10591) Open daily, except Tuesday, April through October, 10a.m.-5p.m.; Open during November, December and March until 4p.m.; During January and February open weekends only. Admission charged.

Lyndhurst, 635 South Broadway, Tarrytown, N.Y. 10591. (914) 631-0046. (pp.30,31) (A National Trust for Historic Preservation property.) Open May through October, Tuesday through Sunday, 10a.m.-5p.m.; January through April and November, weekends only. Admission charged.

Sunnyside, Route 9, Tarrytown, N.Y. 10591. (914) 631-8200. (pp.32–35) (A Historic Hudson Valley property, 150 White Plains Road, Tarrytown, N.Y. 10591.) Open daily, except Tuesday, April through October, 10a.m.-5p.m.; November, December and March until 4p.m.; January through April and November open weekends only. Admission charged.

Philipsburg Manor, Route 9, North Tarrytown, N.Y. 10591. (914) 631-8200. (pp.36,37) (A Historic Hudson Valley property, 150 White Plains Road, Tarrytown, N.Y. 10591.) Open daily except Tuesday, April through October, 10a.m.-5p.m.; November, December and March until 4p.m.; January through April and November open weekends only. Admission charged.

Coe Hall at Planting Fields Arboretum, P.O. Box 58, Oyster Bay, N.Y. 11771. (516) 922-0479. (pp.38–41) Open April through September, Monday to Friday, 1p.m.–3:30p.m. Self-guided tours during the October Fall Flower Show and the December Winter Festival. Admission charge for the mansion is addition to the fee charged for the Arboretum.

Sagamore Hill National Historic Site, 20 Sagamore Hill Road, Oyster Bay, N.Y. 11771. (516) 922-4447. (pp.42,43) Open daily 9:30a.m.-5p.m. Admission charged.

The Vanderbilt Museum, 180 Little Neck Road, Centerport, N.Y. 11721. (516) 262-7888. (pp.44–47) Open daily, except Monday, 10a.m.-5p.m.; November through March open noon–4p.m. Separate admission fees are charged for the Mansion, Marine Museum and Planetarium.

Falaise, Middleneck Road, Port Washington, N.Y. 11050. (516) 883-1612. (pp.52–55) Open May through mid-November, Saturday to Wednesday. Admission charged.

Old Westbury Gardens, Old Westbury Road, Old Westbury, N.Y. 11568. (516) 333-0048. (pp.56–59) Open April through October, Wednesday to Sunday, 10a.m.-5p.m. Admission charged.

New Jersey

Mainstay Inn, 635 Columbia Avenue, Cape May, N.J. 08204. (609) 884-8690. (pp.60–63) Operates as a year-round bed and breakfast inn. Tours of the ground floor are given Saturday, Sunday, Tuesday and Thursday afternoons at 4p.m.

The Abbey, Columbia Avenue and Gurney Street, Cape May, N.J. 08204. (609) 884-4506. (pp.64,65) Operates as a year-round bed and breakfast inn. Tours are given Thursday through Sunday afternoons at 4p.m.

The Queen Victoria, 102 Ocean Street, Cape May, N.J. 08204. (609) 884-8702. (pp.66,67) Operates as a year-round bed and breakfast inn.

Emlen Physick Estate, 1048 Washington Street, Cape May, N.J. 08204. (609) 884-5404. (pp.68–71) Open weekends January through March, with expanded schedules April through December. Admission includes tours of the mansion as well as other buildings on the estate.

Ringwood Manor, Box 1304, Ringwood, N. J. 07456. (201) 962-7031. (pp.72,73) Open May through October, except Monday, 10a.m.-4:30p.m. Entrance fee to Ringwood State Park includes access to the mansion.

Drumthwacket, 354 Stockton Street, Princeton, N.J. 08540. (609) 924-3044. (pp.74,75) Open Wednesdays, noon-2p.m.; and by appointment.

Pennsylvania

Hartwood Acres, 215 Saxonburg Blvd., Pittsburgh, Pa. 15238. (412) 767-9200. (pp.77–79) Open daily except Monday. Admission charged.

Pennsbury Manor, 400 Pennsbury Memorial Road, Morrisville, Pa. 19067. (215) 946-0400. (p.80) Open Tuesday to Saturday 9a.m.–5p.m.; Sunday from noon. Admission fee includes extensive gardens and 15 historic buildings.

The David Bradford House, 175 South Main Street, Washington, Pa. 15301. (412) 222-3604. (pp.81–83) Open May through mid-December, Wednesday to Saturday 11a.m.–4p.m.; Sunday from 1p.m. Admission charged.

Curtin Village, Route 150, Bellefonte, Pa. 16823. (814) 355-1892. (pp.84,85) Open May through October, Tuesday to Saturday 10a.m.–4p.m.; Sunday 1p.m.–5p.m. Admission fee includes the mansion, the restored iron furnace and the village of iron workers' cottages.

Boal Mansion, Route 322, Boalsburg, Pa. 16827. (814) 466-6210. (pp.86–89) Open May, September and October 2p.m.–5p.m.; June through September 10a.m.–5p.m. Admission charge includes the Boal Mansion and Museum and the Christopher Columbus Chapel.

Joseph Priestley House, 472 Priestley Avenue, Northumberland, Pa. 17857. (717) 473-9474. (pp.90,91) Open Tuesday through Saturday, 9a.m.–5p.m; Sunday from noon. Admission charged.

John Harris-Simon Cameron House, 219 S. Front Street, Harrisburg, Pa. 17105. (717) 233-3462. (pp.92,93) Open Monday to Friday 11a.m.–3p.m.; and on the second Sunday of each month 1p.m.–4p.m. Admission charged.

Fort Hunter Mansion, 5300 N. Front Street, Harrisburg, Pa. 17110. (717) 599-5751. (pp.94–97) Open May through December, Tuesday to Saturday 10a.m.–4:30p.m.; Sunday from noon. Admission charged.

Woodford Mansion, 33rd and Dauphin Streets, Philadelphia, Pa. 19132. (215) 229-6115. (pp.98–101) Open daily except Mondays and holidays. Admission charged.*

Cedar Grove, Lansdowne Drive off N. Concourse Drive, Philadelphia, Pa. 19132. (215) 763-8100. (pp.102,103) Open Tuesday to Saturday, 10a.m.–5p.m. Admission charged. *

Strawberry Mansion, 33rd and Dauphin Streets, Philadelphia, Pa. 19132. (215) 228-8364. (pp.104–107) Open Tuesday to Saturday, 10a.m.–5p.m. Admission charged.*

Mount Pleasant, Mount Pleasant Drive, Philadelphia, Pa. 19132. (215) 763-8100. (p.108) Open Tuesday to Sunday, 10a.m.–5p.m. Admission charged.*

Sweetbriar, Fairmount Park West, Philadelphia, Pa. 19132. (215) 222-1333. (p.109) Open March through January, except Tuesdays, 10a.m.–5p.m. Admisison charged.*

Laurel Hill, E. Edgely Drive, Philadelphia, Pa. 19132. (215) 235-1776. (p.110) Open Wednesday to Sunday, 10a.m.–4p.m. Admission charged.*

* These houses, among others, are located in Philadelphia's Fairmount Park. Group tours are available, and all of them can be reached in spring, summer and fall with special trolley bus service from 16th Street and Kennedy Blvd.

Delaware

Nemours, Rockland Road, Wilmington, Delaware 19899. (302) 651-6912. (pp.114–119) Two-hour guided tours are given May through November, Tuesday to Saturday 9a.m., 11a.m.,1p.m. and 3p.m.; Sunday 11a.m., 1p.m. and 3p.m. Admission charged.

Winterthur, Winterthur, Delaware 19735. (302) 654-1548. Or (800) 448-3883. (pp.120–125) Open Tuesday through Saturday, 9a.m.–5p.m.; Sunday from noon. Admission charged.

Hagley Museum, Route 141, Wilmington, Delaware 19807. (302) 658-2400. (pp.120–131) Open daily April through December, 9:30a.m.–4:30p.m.; January through March open weekends only. Admission charged.

George Read II House, 42 The Strand, New Castle, Delaware 19720. (302) 322-8411. (pp.132–135) Open March through December, Tuesday to Saturday 10a.m.–4p.m.; Sunday from noon. Admission charged.

Maryland

Mount Clare, Carroll Park, Baltimore, Maryland 21230. (301) 837-3262. (pp.136,137) Open Tuesday to Friday 10a.m.–4:30p.m.; weekends from noon. Admission charged.

Homewood, 3400 N. Charles Street, Baltimore, Maryland 21218. (301) 338-7654. (pp.138,139) Open all year. Call to check hours.

Hampton National Historic Site, 535 Hampton Lane, Towson, Maryland 21204. (301) 962-0688. (pp.140–143) Grounds are open daily 9a.m.–5p.m.; the mansion is open Monday to Saturday 11a.m.–4p.m.; Sunday from 1p.m. Admission charged.

Hammond-Harwood House, 19 Maryland Avenue, Annapolis, Maryland 21404. (301) 269-1714. (pp.144,145) Open April through October, Tuesday to Saturday 10a.m.–5p.m.; Sunday from 2p.m.; November through March, Tuesday to Saturday 10a.m.–4p.m.; Sunday from 1p.m. Admission charged.

William Paca House, 186 Prince George Street, Annapolis, Maryland 21401. (301) 263-5553. (pp.146–149) Gardens are open May through October, Monday to Saturday 10a.m.–4p.m.; Sundays from noon; and every day May through October, noon–5p.m. The house is open Tuesday to Saturday 10a.m.–4p.m.; Sundays from noon. Admission charged.

District of Columbia

The Octagon, 1799 New York Avenue NW, Washington, D.C. 20006. (202) 638-3105. (pp.150,151) Open weekdays except Monday, 10a.m.–4p.m.; weekends from 1p.m. Admission charged.

Decatur House, 748 Jackson Place NW, Washington, D.C. 20006. (202) 842-0920. (pp.152,153) A property of the National Trust for Historic Preservation, open Tuesday to Friday, 10a.m.–2p.m.; weekends, noon–4p.m. Admission charged.

Woodrow Wilson House, 2340 S Street NW, Washington, D.C. 20008. (202) 673-4034. (pp.154,155) A property of the National Trust for Historic Preservation, open March through December, Tuesday to Sunday, and at weekends in February, 10a.m.–4p.m. Admission charged.

Anderson House, 2118 Massachusetts Avenue NW, Washington, D.C. 20008. (202) 785-2040. (pp.156–160) Open Tuesday to Saturday, 1p.m.–4p.m. The Harold Leonard Stuart Library, a reference collection on the American Revolution, is open weekdays 10a.m.–4p.m.

The George Eastman House (previous page), in Rochester, New York, the former home of the founder of Eastman Kodak, now houses the International Museum of Photography. In East Aurora, New York, the Millard Fillmore House (these pages), home of the thirteenth President, is now a museum. It has been restored, and is furnished as it was when Fillmore moved to the White House in 1850.

The Schuyler Mansion (these pages), in Albany, New York, was finished in 1764 according to designs by Philip Schuyler – a colonial military and political leader. After the British defeat at Saratoga in 1777, General Burgoyne and his staff were held prisoner in the mansion. Three years later a rather more willing guest, Alexander Hamilton, married Schuyler's daughter here, and former president Millard Fillmore was also married in the house in 1858.

The Vanderbilt Mansion (these pages), now the Vanderbilt Mansion National Historic Site, set in a 212-acre estate which overlooks the Hudson River at Hyde Park, New York, was designed by McKim, Mead & White for Frederick William Vanderbilt in 1898. The Vanderbilts could, and often did, entertain as many as thirty guests in their Renaissance dining room (facing page bottom), but they also sometimes dined alone, facing each other across a white expanse of tablecloth.

The Franklin D. Roosevelt Home (these pages) in Hyde Park, New York, is not only the 32nd President's birthplace, but also the place he loved more than any other. Mrs. Roosevelt said of him: "he always felt that this was his home, and he loved the house and the view, the woods, special trees..." His desk in the library (right), and the telephone hotline next to his bed (top right) are reminders of the long hours he worked here while he was President. The elegant comfort of the house is manifest in the dining room (above), the living room (facing page bottom) and the Dresden Room (top), which was redecorated in 1939 for a visit by England's King and Queen, and takes its name from the elegantly wrought Dresden chandelier and mantle set, which were brought over from Germany in 1866. The floral drapes and matching upholstery were part of the redecoration that preceded the royal visit.

States Morris Dyckman's 1804 mansion, Boscobel (these pages), overlooking the Hudson River in Garrison, New York, was nearly destroyed by developers in the 1950s. However, saved through the support of Lila Acheson Wallace – co-founder of *The Reader's Digest* – it was moved, piece by piece, fifteen miles north of its original site. The mansion, considered to be one of the country's finest Federal style houses, is furnished with many period pieces. These include original work by Duncan Phyfe, and Dyckman's own English china, silver and parts of his original library. The beautiful grounds include a thriving apple orchard.

The views from many of the rooms at Boscobel (these pages) are of the dramatic Hudson Highlands, where the Hudson River cuts through the Appalachians to create a scenically spectacular rocky gorge. The house stands near Bear Mountain State Park, and its view to the south is of historic West Point.

Montgomery Place (these pages and overleaf), in Annandale-on-Hudson, New York, was built in 1805 for Janet Livingstone Montgomery, widow of General Richard Montgomery. It was later remodeled by architect Alexander Jackson Davis, who introduced some Classical Revival refinements to the sturdy Federal house, and further landscaped in the mid 19th century by Andrew Jackson Downing, who said of it: "it is one of our oldest improved country seats ... nowhere surpassed in America in point of location, natural beauty, or landscape gardening charms." The jigsaw

puzzle on the sitting room table (facing page bottom) has not been touched since the mansion was opened to the public. The portrait in the entrance hall (above) is of President Andrew Jackson, and General Montgomery's Portrait hangs in the Montgomery Room (overleaf left). Many of the rooms are furnished with family heirlooms. The view from the North Portico is of the Hudson River and Catskill Mountains, giving Montgomery Place a peaceful, scenic setting.

Van Cortlandt Manor (these pages), a 17th-century Dutch patroonship in Croton-on-Hudson, New York, contains family furniture and artifacts produced by craftsmen from the surrounding area. The rooms, all restored to their 1790s appearance, still contain possessions of one of New Amsterdam's original merchant class families. One of the family's community obligations was to provide a Prophet's Chamber (top) for the comfort of circuit-riding preachers. Accurate imitations and early-19th-century flowering bulbs, carefully researched by the Hudson Valley horticulturalists, are beautiful reminders of New York's Dutch heritage flowering still in the gardens of Van Cortlandt Manor.

Lyndhurst (these pages), a Gothic Revival house in Tarrytown, New York, was designed by Alexander Jackson Davis in 1838 for a former New York mayor, William Paulding. He called it "Knoll". It subsequently became the summer home of the railroad millionaire Jay Gould in 1880. The gardens, open lawns and carefully placed shrubs and trees are outstanding examples of Victorian landscaping, and the rose garden (above) contains over 127 varieties of roses.

The rooms at Lyndhurst and its art gallery (bottom) are furnished
in the fashion of the 1880s, when the mansion was Jay Gould's
country retreat. His daughter, Helen Gould, later opened the doors
of Lyndhurst to a wider public and encouraged reading and
dancing parties for young people in her house. After her death, her
sister Anna, Duchess of Talleyrand-Perigord, returned from France
to live at Lyndhurst. When she died, Lyndhurst passed into the
hands of the National Trust.

Sunnyside (these pages), in Tarrytown, New York, was originally a tenant farmer's house on the Philipsburg Manor, but was remodeled in 1835, given Dutch stepped gables and otherwise "fitted up to my own humor" by the author Washington Irving. It was one of the first houses in the area to have running water and a boiler to heat it. Irving made Sleepy Hollow, the setting for the house, famous in his story *The Legend of Sleepy Hollow*. Moreover, the name Van Tassel, also made famous in this story, was the family name of Sunnyside's owners during the eighteenth century. Above: the ice house, where a year-round ice supply was kept.

In Sunnyside (these pages) Washington Irving played the flute in his parlor (facing page top), and shared Hudson River sunsets with his guests through the windows of the dining room (facing page bottom). His nieces' bedroom (top) contains a family field bed with hand-made bobbin lace hangings, and his study (above), where he wrote his biography of George Washington, is full of his personal effects. But of all Irving's possessions, the one he treasured most was this "dear, bright little home."

Philipsburg Manor (these pages), in North Tarrytown, New York, is a restoration of the Upper Mills on the estate of Frederick Flypse or Flypsen, who came to the New World in the early 1650s as Governor Peter Stuyvesant's carpenter. It is preserved in the style of the mid-18th century, its period of greatest prosperity, when tenant farmers brought their corn and wheat here to be ground and shipped toManhattan. The restored rooms of the Manor House (facing page) contain early New York furniture as well as pieces brought from Europe during the Colonial period. They also house fine examples of Dutch Delft ceramics and imported brassware. The twenty-acre site also includes a working gristmill and an 18th-century farm.

Coe Hall (these pages), in Oyster Bay, New York, was one of the jewels of Long Island's Gold Coast when it was built in the 1920s. This English Tudor style house was designed in 1918 by Walker & Gillette for the insurance executive W. R. Coe, who created the 400-acre Planting Fields Arboretum that surrounds it. The interiors, including the Louis XVI reception room (facing page), are furnished with European antiques.

The drawing room (facing page) in Coe Hall (these pages) was a center for family entertainment, but the Den (top) was used extensively for business meetings and managing the estate and its gardens. The dining room (above) was furnished in the style of an English manor house, as are other rooms in the mansion, which were designed by the decorator Charles J. Duveen, who was famous in the 20s as "Charles of London."

Sagamore Hill (these pages), the estate of President Theodore Roosevelt at Oyster Bay, New York, was built in 1885 and remained Roosevelt's home until his death in 1919. His spirit still seems to preside in the house, where his personal taste is represented unchanged in the original furnishings of his parlor (facing page bottom) and in the North Room (top and right), filled with his hunting trophies, flags and books. He said of the house's decoration: "I had to live inside and not outside the house, and while I should have liked to express myself in both, as I had to choose, I chose the former." Of course, some of the furnishings are expressions of his official standing: the President's bedroom (top right) still contains a quilt given to him by the Emperor of Japan. The dining room (right, second from top) is filled with reminders of more quiet family times, and the library (above right), which was his private office, is a shrine to the people he admired, especially his father, whom he called "the best man I ever knew."

The Vanderbilt Museum (these pages) in Centerport, New York, was designed as a country estate by Whitney Warren, the architect of New York's Grand Central Terminal, for his cousin William K. Vanderbilt II. The oak-paneled Organ Room (facing page top) contains an Aeolian Duo-Art pipe organ that can be played manually or automatically – its 1,200 pipes are hidden behind the early 18th-century Aubusson Chinoiserie tapestry on the stairway wall and it could be heard downstairs in the Portuguese Sitting Room (facing page bottom) as Vanderbilt worked at his desk. He also had a desk (above) in his bedroom, which is furnished in the French Empire Style and its distinctive ceiling is decorated with plaster stars, flowers and shells. His personal collection of sea shells and marine science specimens are now housed in a museum wing of the mansion. The complex also includes one of America's largest planetariums, comprising a sixty-foot sky theater and an exhibit-filled gallery.

Vanderbilt's mahogany bedroom suite (above) in the Vanderbilt Mansion and Museum (these pages) is a copy of one made for Napoleon, while Mrs. Vanderbilt's bedroom (right) is in the Louis XVI Style. Some of the rooms are named for famous guests who slept in them, including the Norwegian figure skater Sonja Henie (below left), and the Dutchess of Windsor (below right). The corner fireplace (facing page) in the dining room is hooded with a mantle bearing the Vanderbilt coat of arms. The dining room itself is decorated with brown and turquoise Portuguese tiles and, like the mansion's exterior, has a distinctively Mediterranean look. The house, originally called "Eagle's Nest," was a small cottage at first, but during the 1920s and '30s it was expanded into the famous, elegant, formal home we now know. The original museum wing was built to house Vanderbilt's own natural history collection.

Honestum Praetulit Utili

Knole (these pages and overleaf), the Old Westbury, New York, estate of Esmond Bradley Martin, was designed by Thomas Hastings in 1903. The house sits on top of a hill surrounded by thirty-three landscaped acres. Its most dramatic feature is the three-story oval rotunda (facing page bottom and above) over the entrance hall. The mansion is furnished with an eclectic collection of furniture and artifacts from Europe and the Orient, including a rare Chippendale commode among 17th- and 18th-century pieces in the drawing room (top right and overleaf right). The Adam Room (top) is furnished with 18th-century antiques, as is the breakfast room (overleaf left top). The dining room (overleaf left bottom) is in the Queen Anne Style. The Solarium (right) offers views of the formal French and Italian gardens, terraced on several levels behind the house. Of the hundreds of mansions that once lined Long Island's Gold Coast, Knole is one of less than a dozen which are still private residences.

Falaise (these pages), a French-style manor at Sands Point, New York, was built for Captain Harry F. Guggenheim in 1923. Among its many rooms is the one (top right) used by Charles Lindbergh to write his book, *We*. Left: the three-story entrance hall, (above) the courtyard entrance and (top left) the Garden Room.

Falaise (these pages), named for a town in Normandy, is furnished in the subdued and elegant style of the 1920s and '30s – a time when its owner was active in the Guggenheim business and promoting the cause of aviation in America. Working with his third wife, Alicia Patterson, he also helped establish *Newsday* as one of the country's great daily newspapers, an activity that made Falaise an important gathering place for influential people in the pre-World War II years.

Westbury House (these pages), the former country estate of John S. Phipps in Old Westbury, New York, is decorated with 18th-century antiques and hung with paintings by Joshua Reynolds, Henry Raeburn, Thomas Gainsborough, John Constable and John Singer Sargent. It is the centerpiece of the Old Westbury Gardens, a 100-acre expanse of formal gardens, that includes a romantic garden rotunda called the "Temple of Love" (above). The fireplace in the dining room (facing page) is decorated with intricately carved swags hung above it on the oak-paneled wall.

Mr. Phipps' dressing room (facing page top) in Westbury House (these pages), subsequently a guest room, is hung with English hand-blocked wallpaper and furnished with late-18th-century carved mahogany pieces. The White Drawing Room (facing page bottom and top left), with its Waterford cut-glass chandeliers, was used for family tea. The 18th-century mantle over its fireplace was made in England, and the one in the master bedroom (above right) was designed to complement its Chippendale furniture. The Adam Room (top right) contains an antique mantlepiece, and in the Chippendale guest room (above left), the gilt overmantle is arranged in a pagoda design.

Since its days as Jackson's Clubhouse, a gentlemen's gambling establishment, the Mainstay Inn (these pages), Cape May, New Jersey, has been carefully maintained in its Victorian elegance as an inn, and guests are very pleasantly accommodated around the Victorian walnut table in the dining room (facing page) of an evening. A local newspaper, *Ocean Wave*, accurately described Mainstay Inn as "symmetrical in its proportions, airy and cheerful in its appointments, and furnished in that unpretentious elegance so foreign to mansions of the shoddy order."

The 1872 Mainstay Inn (these pages) in Cape May, New Jersey, was originally a gambling establishment – a period in its history which is recalled by the antique piano and gaming table still in situ in the drawing room (above). Its front parlor (facing page), completely restored to its original high Victorian Style, is now the room where afternoon teas are served to the guests of the inn and, indeed, to any others who drop in to look at the details of this house.

The Abbey (these pages), in Cape May, New Jersey, was originally an 1869 Gothic villa built as a summer home for Pennsylvanian coal baron, John McCreary. The Second Empire style cottage his son built nearby was later united with it to form The Abbey Inn. Its parlor (top) and dining room (above) are furnished with Victorian antiques, and the Abbey's music room (facing page) is one of the most delightful rooms at the inn, a veritable magnet for lovers of Victoriana. Indeed, Cape May is a historic town, containing a number of magnificent Victorian homes, and is one of the few to have been designated a National Landmark.

Cape May's Queen Victoria Inn (these pages), an 1881 seaside villa, is furnished with authentic period pieces, including fine examples of Roycroft furniture in the parlor (left and above).

The Emlen Physick Estate (these pages) is possibly Cape May's finest Victorian treasure. It was designed in 1878 by Frank Furness for the son of Dr. Philip Syng Physick, one of the first American surgeons. Its restoration has been continuous since 1973, and a large number of the original furnishings have joined other valuable pieces donated by individuals and institutions. The house is now a far cry from the vacant "haunted house" it had been in the '60s. MAC, the Mid-Atlantic Center for the Arts, was formed to save this beautiful house from the wrecker's ball, and it is now home to MAC's resident summer stock company, Theater By The Sea.

69

The eighteen-room Physick Estate (these pages) was the first high-Victorian house built in Cape May, and it kept pace with changing fashions in interior design, acquiring new forms of ornamentation, particularly some new, romantic fireplaces, up until Dr. Physick's death. But now the rooms he knew are frozen in time, preserved as a fascinating reminder of the days when Emlen Physick lived the life of a country gentleman here in the height of turn-of-the-century fashion.

Ringwood Manor (these pages) in Passaic County, New Jersey, was built by the family of Abram S. Hewitt, the son-in-law of Peter Cooper and his partner in the Ringwood Company iron business. The house is furnished with American artifacts gathered by the Cooper and Hewitt families during the 19th century. In 1782, after Erskine Hewitt's death at Ringwood in 1780, George Washington planted a tree at his graveside on the property – a gesture of appreciation for the work Erskine had done preparing maps to aid Washington's military campaigns.

The official residence of the Governor of New Jersey, Drumthwacket (these pages), in Princeton, was built in 1835 by Charles Olden, himself a New Jersey Governor. He chose the Greek Revival Style after living in New Orleans, Louisiana, where he had been very impressed with the antebellum plantation houses there. Today the mansion hosts State functions and charitable events. The site is historically very important, having been so close to the battlegrounds of Princeton, Trenton and Monmouth.

Clayton (this page), the Pittsburgh, Pennsylvania, home of steel baron Henry Clay Frick, is soon to be opened as a museum with most of its original 1892 furnishings intact. Hartwood Acres (facing page), the Tudor mansion of John Lawrence, takes advantage of its scenic setting in Pittsburgh to recreate a charming corner of England's Cotswold region. Its Great Hall (facing page bottom), with its 1620 carved oak fireplace and antique Georgian furniture, is a classic example of Jacobean elegance. Perhaps the most unexpected feature of the room is a rope elevator to carry logs up from the basement – it is concealed behind the paneling on the right hand side of the fireplace. The room also contains a pipe organ moved from the childhood home of Mrs. Lawrence, the daughter of industrialist William Flinn.

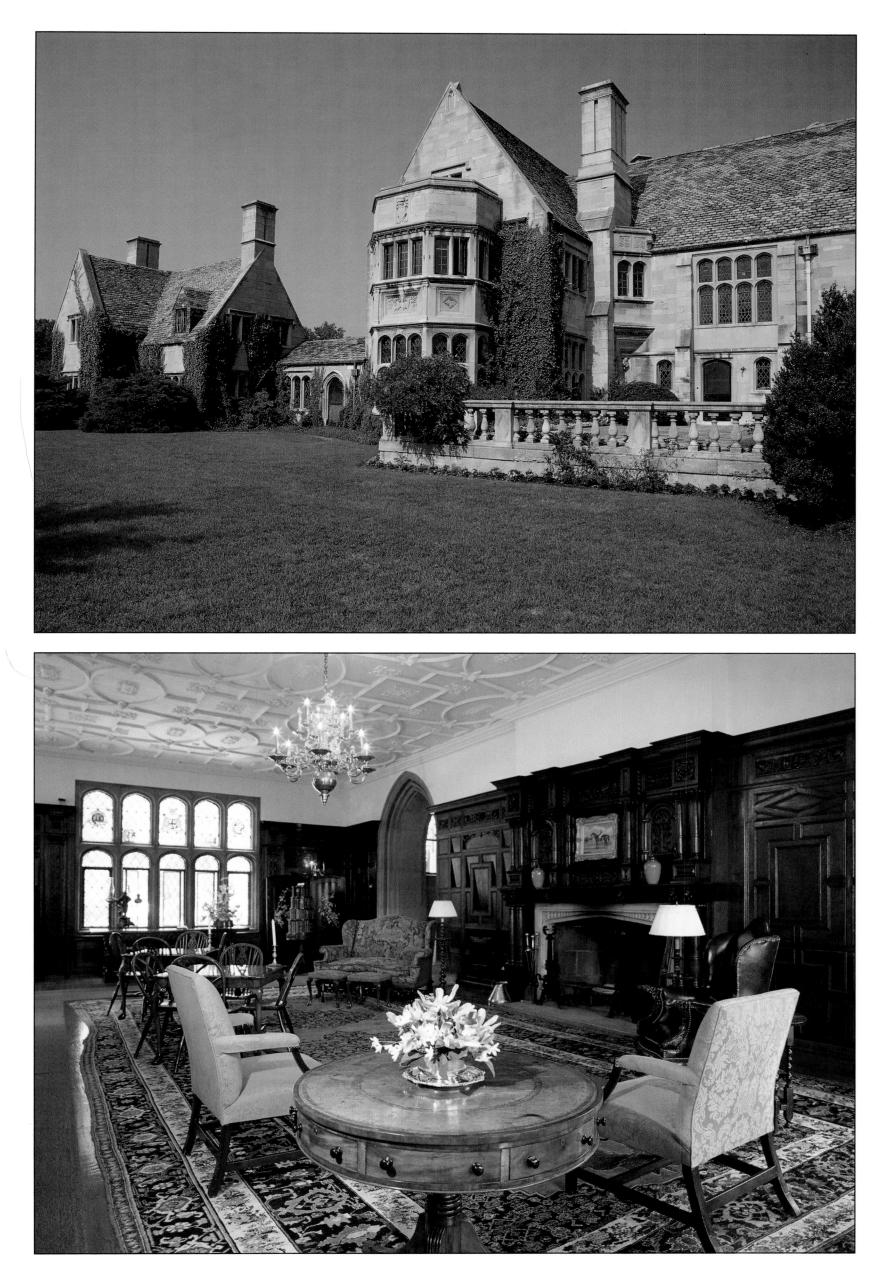

The Steinway grand piano in the Great Hall (facing page, above and top right) in Hartwood Acres (these pages), was custom-made for Mrs. Lawrence. It and the other furnishings in the room are Flinn family heirlooms. The Georgian green and gilt dining room (below) is perhaps the most formal room in the house. It contains examples of the Lawrence's collections of Chinese export porcelain, English silver and Sheffield plate, and its Chippendale side table features an unusual marble top embedded with fossils. Other rooms in the mansion have been virtually untouched since it was a private home. The surrounding 620-acre estate includes a wildlife sanctuary and a picturesque complex of stable buildings.

Pennsbury Manor (this page) in Morrisville, Pennsylvania, was the Georgian country home of William Penn, whose statue (left) still stands guard there. The house was originally built in 1699, and was reconstructed on its original foundations in 1938.

The David Bradford House (this page), in Washington, Pennsylvania, was built in 1788, by David Bradford, a prominent lawyer who was a key figure in the 1791 Western Pennsylvania rebellion against an excise tax on whiskey. His support of the rebels eventually forced him leave his home and relocate his large family in Spanish territory.

Most of the interior decorations and furnishings in the David Bradford House (these pages) were carried across the mountains from the East, but the exterior of the Georgian mansion is built with locally quarried stone. Despite the fact that this house was one of the first buildings to be constructed in Washington when it was on the edge of the wild frontier, the extraordinary elegance of the house would have assured it showplace status even in the later, more secure days of Colonial Philadelphia. The house is now bordered by a state liquor store and a bar – appropriate neighbors for the house of a man who fought the 1791 excise tax on whiskey proposed by Alexander Hamilton and enforced by Congress.

The Roland Curtin Mansion (these pages) in Bellefonte, Pennsylvania, was built in 1830 by Roland Curtin, the owner and founder of the Eagle Ironworks, which, like the mansion and ironworkers' village, has been carefully restored. Curtin was an Irish immigrant who, while training for the priesthood in Paris, was forced to flee the Reign of Terror there. His Federal style mansion, with many of the family's original furnishings still intact in its fifteen rooms, reflects the life styles of Curtin family members who lived here for 150 years. Most of the furnishings in the house, however, are not original to it and date from the late Empire period.

The Boal Mansion (these pages), in Boalsburg, Pennsylvania, was begun in 1789 and expanded by nine successive generations of the Boal family. It includes a 16th-century chapel (facing page bottom and right) built in Spain by Christopher Columbus' family. Among the relics in the chapel are a Spanish admiral's desk and a cross of the type used by Spanish explorers to plant in the ground of new-found territories in the name of the Spanish king. Also in the chapel hangs a 1535 painting, "The Descent from the Cross," by the Flemish master Ambrosius Benson. Having fought the British in Ireland in the late 18th century, David Boal was forced to flee the country and was carried to ship and safety in the chest that stands in the hallway (below).

The ballroom (facing page bottom) in the Boal Mansion (these pages) was added in 1898 when the family farm became the family estate. The parlor (top) and dining room (above) reflect the refined life style of a remarkable family. A museum on the estate contains military and domestic relics dating from medieval times to the present and tracing the history and exploits of the Boal family. The house also contains documents and personal effects which belonged to the Columbus family.

Pneumatic Trough, reproduction—in this 18th century jury-large pan of set in which inverted bottles full of water could be supported outside the trough were set into the inverted bottles in the trough by glass tubes and were caught and held there.

Compound burning glass, replica of an original glass, owned by Joseph Priestley at Northumberland and now in the Dickinson College Collection. Joseph Priestley first collected oxygen in the 1770's by heating mercuric oxide with a burning glass and collecting the air which was given off. In the 18th century burning glasses provided reliable sources of heat for chemical experiments by focusing the sun's rays on an object. Joseph Priestley often used a burning glass in his experiments.

Joseph Priestley, the chemist who discovered oxygen, built his house (these pages) in Northumberland, Pennsylvania, in 1794. Among the experiments conducted in his laboratory (facing page bottom left and right) were some probing the nature of electricity – overseen jointly with his friend, Benjamin Franklin, whose portrait hangs in the dining room (top). Above: the kitchen, and (facing page top) the living room.

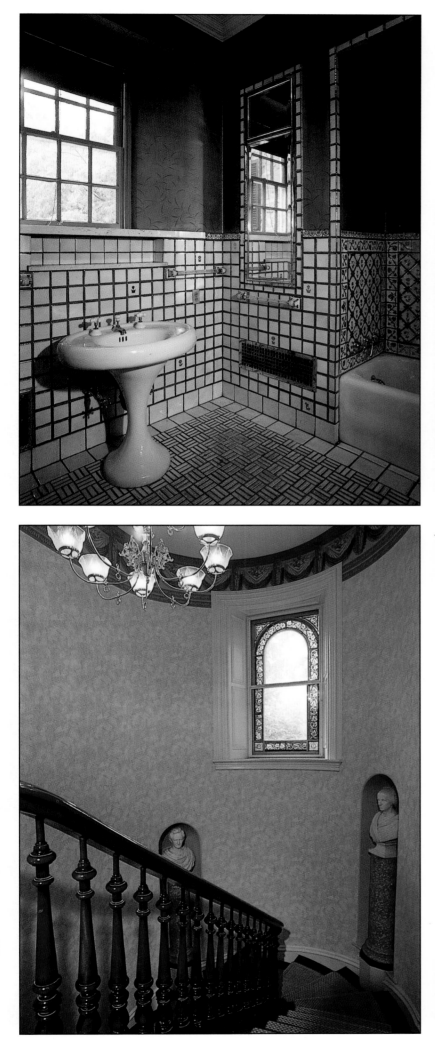

The John Harris-Simon Cameron House (these pages), home of the founder of Harrisburg, Pennsylvania, was later owned by Simon Cameron, an influential politician whose bust, portraying him as a Roman patrician, stands in the stair hall (above left), the walls of which are papered to simulate marble. An Art Deco bathroom (top left) was added by an even later owner in 1920, and the original hand-painted wallpaper on the walls of the Solarium (top right) has been painstakingly restored. When the drawing room (above right), was remodeled, its floor was lowered to accommodate the high Victorian Style in which it was furnished.

The Federal style Fort Hunter Mansion (these pages), in Harrisburg, Pennsylvania, was built in 1814 by Archibald McAllister on the site of a British fort established during the French and Indian War. From the start, the farm was the center of an important frontier village. Its view over the Susquehanna River and the Blue Mountains beyond gave it a strategically advantageous position. Its fine entrance hall (above left and above right) and elliptical staircase (above left) act as a introduction to the rooms, which are furnished in styles ranging from Early American to Empire and Victorian, tracing the history of the families that owned and loved it.

Memories of the children who grew up in Fort Hunter (these pages) abound, brought to the fore by their many belongings which are still in the house, side by side with those of their parents and relatives. The bedrooms (facing page and bottom left), even the closets (below left) seem to be waiting for them to come home – as does the curious-looking bath (bottom left and facing page bottom) sitting out in apparent readiness. The charming and historic, landscaped thirty-seven-acre grounds of Fort Hunter – still containing buttonwood trees dating from William Penn's time – include a 19th-century boxwood garden and an herb garden. The peaceful setting for the house, riddled with meandering paths and picturesque picnic areas, overlooks a bend in the Susquehanna River.

The Woodford Mansion (these pages), in Philadelphia's Fairmount Park, was built by merchant William Coleman in 1756. It contains the Naomi Wood Collection of Colonial household equipment – considered to be the best collection of its kind in America. The second floor study (top) is furnished entirely with pieces made from New England maple, ranging from the candlesticks to the panel-backed settee.

The kitchen (above) in Woodford Mansion (these pages), Philadelphia, contains a rare collection of Pennsylvanian Dutch ware and furniture. The master bedroom (top), along with many other rooms in the house, combines furnishings made from fine fabrics with elegant pastel wallcoverings and carved woodwork to create a strong sense of gentility. The dining room (facing page), furnished with Hepplewhite and Sheraton pieces, is an unusual example of the city's fashion during its years as the national capital. Benjamin Franklin and other important dignitaries often dined here, and the mansion is virtually unchanged since those days.

Cedar Grove (these pages), Philadelphia, a Quaker farmhouse, dates back to 1740, but was subsequently altered fifty years after that date. Its unusually fine collection of Jacobean, Queen Anne, William and Mary, Chippendale and Federal furniture was assembled through five generations of the Paschall-Morris family to whom Cedar Grove was home.

The 1789 Strawberry Mansion (these pages and overleaf), Philadelphia, was built by the lawyer Judge William Lewis. It was expanded by Judge Joseph Hemphill in the 1920s with the addition of classical wings, and eventually the site was acquired by William Penn in an historic land swap with Swedish settlers. The mansion's rooms are furnished in Empire, Regency and Federal styles, appropriately representing distinct phases in its history, and recalling times when the most prominent politicians of the early 19th century were frequent visitors.

Mount Pleasant (this page), a monument to the detail and elegance of the Georgian Style, was built by a Philadelphian privateer, Captain John MacPherson, in 1761. John Adams said it was "the most elegant seat in Pennsylvania." Benedict Arnold was one of its owners, but his conviction for treason prevented him from ever actually living in the house. The Chippendale furniture in Mount Pleasant was made in Philadelphia. Its nearby neighbor, Sweetbriar (facing page), was built in 1797 and is one of the most perfect examples of the American adaptation of architectural ideas from England's Adam brothers.

Laurel Hill (above), a Georgian house built in 1767, has been home to many prominent Philadelphians, including Mayor Samuel Shoemaker. Among the period pieces in the Laurel Hill furniture collection is an 1808 pianoforte and an 1831 harp. Baleroy (facing page), said by many to be haunted, is also decorated in the style of its past. The drawing room (facing page top) is as it would have been during the 18th century, and the Chippendale bed in the master bedroom (facing page bottom left) was the model for one in the White House.

The Carriage House (below) of Baleroy (these pages), Old Chestnut Hill, Philadelphia, includes, among other artifacts, a chair Napoleon took with him into exile – but the chairs in the dining room (bottom) have a peculiarly American significance: they were used by the signatories of the Declaration of Independence. The reception room (facing page), filled with Philadelphian Chippendale furniture, contains a lowboy whose matching piece is in the map room at the White House. The portrait is of William, Lord Craven, a Lord Mayor of London and Prince of Bohemia.

Alfred I. duPont named his Wilmington, Delaware, estate (these pages and overleaf) for Nemours, his family's ancestral home in France. This Louis XVI-style château was designed by Carrère and Hastings and built in 1910. The formal gardens (facing page top) create a vista from the house and include a maze garden designed around a pool (facing page bottom) surmounted by a gold-painted sculpture of "Achievement" by Henri Crenier. Either side of this statue are two tritons, the bases of which are sculpted with the face of Neptune. Roman-style sunken gardens (below) beyond a colonnade based on designs by Alfred duPont and Gabriel Massena, were added in 1932. The white Carrara marble sculptures in the sunken gardens are by Charles Sarrabezolles. The lavish interiors of Nemours, beginning at the reception hall door (right), are noted for their classical detail. Among its 102 rooms are the conservatory (overleaf right top) and the morning room (overleaf right bottom). Its grand staircase (overleaf left) is dominated by a stained glass window bearing the duPont family's coat of arms.

Every room in Nemours (these pages), from the reception hall (below) to the library (bottom) and dining room (facing page), speaks of the elegant and dignified life style of its inhabitants. The mansion is furnished throughout with rare European and American pieces of furniture, priceless rugs, tapestries and works of art. Nearly all of the furnishings were personally collected by Alfred I. duPont on his travels in America and abroad.

Winterthur (these pages), near Wilmington, Delaware, the estate of Henry Francis duPont, dates from 1865, but was enlarged in 1929 to hold Mr. duPont's collection of American antiques. The Queen Anne dining room (bottom) contains woodwork from a New England mansion, and the Montmorenci staircase (facing page top) was formerly in a North Carolina house.

The Port Royal Parlor (facing page bottom) in Winterthur (these pages), and the entrance hall (facing page top) contain Philadelphia Chippendale furniture. Other rooms, such as the Sheraton Room (bottom), the Albany Room (below right) and Cecil's Room (right) reflect the changing styles from 1650 to 1850.

The Chinese Room (facing page top) in Winterthur (these pages), Delaware, is hung with wallpaper made in China in about 1770. It depicts scenes from daily life in an Oriental village and provides a suitable frame for the room's furnishings, which are generally Western adaptations of Chinese pieces – examples of what was known at the time as the "Chinese taste." The Flock Room (facing page bottom) is also named for its wallcovering, and the Wentworth Room (top) and the Federal style duPont Dining Room (above) are among nearly 200 exquisitely furnished rooms in Winterthur.

Eleutherian Mills (facing page top), built by E.I. duPont in 1803, is the centerpiece of Hagley (these pages), a 230-acre park on the Brandywine River near Wilmington, Delaware. Hagley is the site of the first duPont black powder works, established in 1801, and contains industrial exhibits as well as the Georgian style mansion, which was home to five generations of duPonts. The grounds, filled with trees and flowering shrubs, include a classical garden which charmingly incorporates ruins of old mill buildings, and a formal French Renaissance garden.

Eleuthère Irénée duPont, who gave his name to Eleutherian Mills (these pages), lived in this mansion until his death in 1834. It was enlarged and altered by several successive generations, and, accordingly, the period furnishings represent Federal, Empire and Victorian decorative styles. In Irénée and Sophie's room (top) a mahogany crib stands next to the bed, and a two-volume *La Sainte Bible*, published in Lyon, France, lies on the night table. Draped over the settee in the Daughters' Room (above), which lies adjacent to the Blue Room (facing page top), lies the pair of gloves which Eleuthera wore to a ball given in honor of General Lafayette, held during his visit to the house in 1824.

Portraits of the duPonts are found throughout Eleutherian Mills (these pages). One of them, in the formal parlor (facing page top), is of E.I. duPont, who settled here partly because of the large French-speaking population in the area. The family's French heritage is evidenced throughout the house. The dining room (above) wallpaper was imported from France, but is block-printed with North American scenes. Facing page bottom: the morning room, and, opposite it, the parlor (top).

The George Read II House (these pages) in New Castle, Delaware, was built in 1804 by the prominent lawyer of that name, who was determined to create the grandest home in the state. It was restored in 1985 and furnished with an unusually fine collection of antique pieces, including the locally-made clock in Mrs. Read's bedroom (facing page top left). The original three-part windows in the rear parlor (facing page bottom) open outward from the bottom.

The renovation of the George Read II House (these pages), which took place between 1981 and 1985, has restored it to the days when guests of the Reads were served tea in the front parlor (facing page top) and kitchen staff were summoned to various parts of the house by a series of bells in the kitchen (below left). In 1926, the basement tap room (bottom) was installed to accommodate less formal entertainments than those generally held in the dining room (facing page bottom). Mrs. Read's bedroom (left) is furnished as she left it, right down to the hatboxes in her closet (below).

Mount Clare (these pages) was the 1754 home of Charles Carroll in Baltimore, Maryland. The Waterford chandelier and crystal, along with the Sheraton, Chippendale, Hepplewhite and Duncan Phyfe furniture in the dining room (facing page bottom), are original to the house. Carroll's office (facing page center left) was where he sat for his portrait – Charles Wilson Peale's paintings of Carroll and his wife hang in the drawing room (facing page top). Facing page bottom right: the hallway case clock, made in Philadelphia in 1780, and (facing page bottom left) the Carroll master bedroom.

The 1800 Federal mansion, Homewood (these pages), in Baltimore, Maryland, has been lovingly restored by Johns Hopkins University after detailed research. For example, the old Siena-style marbling in the dining room (facing page bottom) was reproduced from a chanced-on fragment of original baseboard. Among the many exquisite features of the drawing room (top), the draped blue silk curtains, based on early 19th-century designs by Pierre de la Mésangère, are perhaps foremost. In the back parlor (above left), the mantle and moldings are simpler, and less formal still is the office (above right).

Hampton (these pages), in Towson, Maryland, is one of the largest Georgian houses in America. The estate was the country seat of the Ridgely family – merchants and planters for two centuries – and its thirty-three rooms are furnished to reflect the different life styles of the family. The drawing room (facing page), the most formal of them, is furnished in the style of the 1830s, whereas the master bedchamber (above right) reflects the style of 1790, when the mansion was built. The "white curtain room" (right), a guest bedchamber, was popular among Ridgely friends as a honeymoon suite.

The dining room (facing page) at Hampton (these pages) has been restored to its 1820s appearance. The chairrail and doors have been painted to simulate mahogany. The music room (above), furnished in Victorian fashion, contains a harp made in England in 1817. The parlor (top) was a family favorite because of its views of the terraced gardens, and the estate is particularly noted for its collection of specimen trees – the formal gardens are among the best remaining examples of 19th-century landscaping in America.

The Georgian Hammond-Harwood House (these pages), in Annapolis, Maryland, is decorated and furnished as it was in 1774, when it was new. The wood carving throughout the house, especially in the dining room (above), is exquisite. The original owner of the mansion, Mathias Hammond, became a member of the Provincial Assembly at the age of twenty-five, and since his time the house has been home to many prominent families, including its last owners, the Harwoods, who lived and entertained here for seventy-five years.

145

The William Paca House (these pages), in Annapolis, was built for a former governor of Maryland in 1765. It is surrounded by a two-acre formal garden stepped on five terraces, containing ponds and a small wilderness garden. This thirty-seven-room Georgian mansion has been restored to its former elegance and today incorporates meeting rooms and modern amenities for use as a conference center. In the early part of the 20th century the house was attached to a hotel, which has since been demolished. It was saved from the wrecker's ball by local citizens in 1965, and today recaptures the feeling of pre-Revolutionary days when Annapolis was one of America's most important trading centers. William Paca, who built the house, was a Governor of Maryland during the Revolutionary period, and a signatory of the Declaration of Independence.

Many of the rooms, including the master bedroom (facing page), dining room (top) and parlor (above) of the William Paca House (these pages), Maryland, are furnished with museum pieces in mid-18th-century style. The rooms, which are sometimes used for overnight guests, are also characterized by an unmistakable 18th-century ambiance, making the house a unique setting for functions of the U.S. State Department and the State of Maryland.

The drawing room (facing page top) of the 1800 Octagon (these pages), Washington, D.C., built for Col. John Tayloe III, contains an English Coade stone mantelpiece. Facing page bottom: the dining room with its Scottish Chippendale breakfront, and (above) the oval staircase, spiraling upwards for three floors. Left: the Treaty Room, so called because it was the room in which President James Madison signed the 1812 Treaty of Ghent.

The Federal style rooms of Decatur House (these pages), a block away from the White House in Washington, D.C., are furnished in a style that would have been familiar to Commodore Stephen Decatur, who commissioned Benjamin Henry Latrobe to design the house in 1816. The rooms representing the Victorian period were created for the Beale family, who lived in the house on Lafayette Square from 1871. Other residents have included Henry Clay and Martin Van Buren. Perhaps the most prominent piece in the South Drawing Room (below) is its magnificent Steinway grand piano, but the grand Victorian style gives way to comfort in the morning room (above left). Throughout the house the parquet flooring is magnificent, but, in the North Drawing Room (facing page), the circular design of Californian parquet, inlaid with state seal of California, is particularly splendid. The dining room (left) still has an intimate atmosphere – the Decaturs used it to entertain family and close friends. In the first-floor bedroom (above) is the 1770 bed which belonged to Commodore Decatur's parents.

On Washington's Embassy Row, the house (these pages) that was the home of former president Woodrow Wilson for the last four years of his life is filled with mementoes of his career, including the desk (above) he used whilst he was President of Princeton University. The bedroom (above right) contains most of the furnishings from his room at the White House, and the library (below) is filled with his personal books and papers. In fact, the dining room (right) and the drawing room (facing page bottom) are just some of the rooms that are furnished with original family belongings. The house is preserved in the state in which Edith Wilson bequeathed it to the National Trust on her death in 1961. She said of it in her 1938 book *My Memoirs*, "I found an unpretentious, comfortable, dignified house, fitted to the needs of a gentleman's home." And so do its visitors today.

The former Washington, D.C., home of Ambassador Larz Anderson, Anderson House (these pages and overleaf) is now the headquarters of the Society of Cincinnati, whose members are the male descendants of officers in the Continental Army and Navy. It was founded in 1783 by General Henry Knox, whose portrait hangs in the ballroom (top and above). The English parlor (facing page), the French parlor (overleaf left), the dining room (overleaf right) and the Solarium (following page) all contain fine antiques and architectural details that belie the fact the house was built in 1905.

INDEX